The Lesson of the Lark

Celebrating the Centennial of the Nineteenth Amendment of the United States Constitution

Written by Laura Knight Cobb & Illustrated by Maya James

The target audience for this work is children ages 10-16. The reading level and vocabulary complexity have been strategically structured in a manner that will lead to differentiation within the creation of lessons.

It is intended to be rigorous, while also maintaining a developmentally appropriate balance. The learning objectives can be independently modified in order to achieve success for every learner.

In addition, this work and instructional materials have been aligned to the Common Core State Standards for use with students from 4th grade through 10th grade.

MISSION POINT PRESS

Published by Mission Point Press
2554 Chandler Rd.
Traverse City, MI 49686
(231) 421-9513
www.MissionPointPress.com

ISBN: 978-1-943995-85-1
Library of Congress Control Number: 2018953809

Printed in the United States of America.

Contents

Dedication

This book is dedicated to all women, young ladies, and girls who have come before me, and all who will live on long after I am gone.

It is with great respect that I share this story with the sincere desire that all men and boys who read this will be enlightened, as well as touched, by this work. It is my hope that their consciences will guide them to see women as strong and powerful beings who bring the light of peace and balance to the world.

As we go about our busy lives, we must remember that the Golden Rule includes the entire human race. Imagine a world where mothers, daughters, grandmothers, granddaughters, sisters, aunts, and nieces are all subservient to men. What if women had absolutely no opinions, thoughts or beliefs of their own? The blessings that women bring to this Earth and mankind are immeasurable.

It is my hope that the *Lesson of the Lark* will awaken us all to the continued obligation of attaining equal rights. Help is still needed in bringing collective awareness, acceptance, and advocacy into the hearts of society. Through this action, change can, and will, evolve into a more equitable future for our daughters and granddaughters. This book is an invitation to celebrate the centennial anniversary and the creation of the Nineteenth Amendment.

It was an honor to collaborate with illustrator Maya James to create the blended vision for this work. Over a decade ago, it was my pleasure to be Maya's fourth grade teacher, and it is now a privilege to see the independent and creative woman she has become.

Thanks to Linda Jarkey and Beth Hoseney for their editing expertise. Special thanks to Susan Cobb for facilitating distribution and promotion, Elijah Cobb for web design and marketing assistance, and Jeffrey Cobb for being a "sounding board" of steadfast encouragement.

Finally, I dedicate this book to my daughter, Arianna, who at sixteen is an insightful and strong-willed young lady. Her light shines as a beacon of both brilliance and sensitivity.

Preface

The seeds of justice for women were planted in New York, on a mid-July day in 1848. Later known as the Seneca Falls Convention, this event propelled the vision for equality, and launched the inception of the Nineteenth Amendment. More than 300 women convened to establish the very first women's rights movement. It was conceived by Lucretia Mott, a Quaker, and Elizabeth Stanton, an abolitionist. Together, they organized the first public discussions regarding the social and civil conditions of women in the United States.

During the first day of the convention, the "Declaration of Sentiments and Grievances" was recited. This treatise closely paralleled the same call for justice as the Declaration of Independence. It brought forth the need for women's rights to be heard, and inspired women to rise up, organize, and petition for liberty.

On the second day of the convention, an invitation was extended to men. More than 40 men were present, including the famous African American abolitionist, Frederick Douglass. The Declaration of Sentiments and Grievances was then officially adopted and signed by the assembly. This resolution marked the beginning of the women's suffrage movement in America.

Following the convention, Stanton and Mott gained momentum with Susan B. Anthony and countless other activists to raise public awareness. They did so through marches, peaceful protests, and by lobbying the government to grant voting rights for women. After lengthy battles, they emerged victorious with the adoption of the Nineteenth Amendment, which was passed by Congress on June 4th, 1919. Finally, it was ratified, and officially adopted into law on August 18th, 1920. American women were now constitutionally protected with the right to vote. After almost a century of protest, the voices of women would no longer be silenced.

Yet, a century later, and after more than 200 years of continued struggles, there is still an urgent need to further equalize the rights of women with those of men. The United States Constitution does NOT guarantee equal rights for women. In fact, since 1923, activists have been trying to pass the Equal Rights Amendment (ERA), which states, "Equality of rights under the law shall not be denied or abridged by the United States or by any state on account of gender." The ERA makes discrimination against women unconstitutional, and prohibits legal distinctions between gender when pertaining to property, employment, and any other legal bias or prejudices by contrast.

According to the Equal Rights Coalition, 96 percent of Americans believe that the ERA has already been passed! This is one reason why the gender pay gap still remains. Currently, women make 78 cents for every dollar earned by a man. Furthermore, African-American women earn only 64 cents, and Latinas a mere 53 cents compared to white males. Over 75 percent of elderly Americans living in poverty are women. Women are earning 60 percent of all college degrees, and still hold less potential for promotional advancement than male college graduates.

The inequities are clear: Women make up 51 percent of our population. Today, a mere 23% of United States Senators, and 19% of United States Congressmen, are women. Our governmental representatives hold the power to make the needed changes. In 1972, the ERA was passed by both the Senate and the House of Representatives. It was then sent to each state for ratification. It was given a 7-year deadline. In the first year, 30 states had ratified; at the end of the deadline 35 had ratified. In order for it to become part of the constitution they required 38. In the end, they fell only 3 states short.

The future depends upon the commitment of ALL citizens; women and men, boys and girls, to be awakened and take action against this blatant discrimination. We must work together to raise awareness, and pass legislation to improve the economic, political, legal, civil, diplomatic, and social conditions for women not only in the United States, but world-wide. This call must include men. Most importantly, it begins with our sons.

We're now at a precipice of change. As more discussion and attention are being brought into the light concerning gender inequality, occupational segregation, violence against women, trafficking, harassment, and discrimination, the skin of oppression for women has begun its shedding process.

Now is the time to acknowledge that the old accepted norms of society are not, and clearly have not been, morally acceptable. As new norms are unveiled, the lines between right and wrong are more easily distinguishable. Our moral compasses can be reset with the realization that we're all connected, and are here to support one another, regardless of gender, color, orientation, faith, or economic status.

This new era is humanity's awakening! As it unfolds, it extends to each of us the opportunity to see our true connectedness and accept one another with impartial unity. With this mindset, we will cultivate a deeper sense of both empathy and inclusion. In doing so, the sprouts of equality will push their way up towards the light, and through the turmoil and strife that society has created.

Out of humanity's fragmentation will emerge a more progressive clarity for the future. Soon enough, the glorious winds of change will greet us with songs of unity. Then we will stand together, side by side in solidarity, once and for all as equals. When this happens, a great reconciliation will occur enabling us all to flourish. Just as it did in the garden, we will once again live in a world of balance, joy, and beauty. This day can be made reality, but it must first begin within each of our hearts...

*A*girl peered into a garden,
A lark sweetly sang, "Where have you been?"
A locked iron gate stood before her,
"I'm here to lift mankind—let me in."

The girl hoisted her starched-white petticoat.
She'd been summoned and given a light.
"Please open this gate," she pleaded,
"I'm here to bring change — make things right."

*T*he lark then eyed a gardener
Who was planting his seeds with great pride.
"To enter, a promise must be kept:
Teach others—their conscience is their guide."

The gardener gave a wink of assurance,
Wiped his brow, for the time had arrived.
He lifted a bent key from his pocket,
Held her elbow, and led her inside.

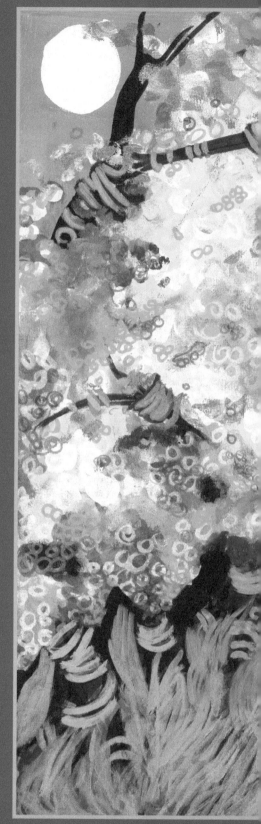

As her mud-caked boots passed the threshold
She glowed a magnificent hue;
Enchanted by fragrant blossoms, and vines,
Her cheeks misted by waterfall's dew.

The gardener's eyes widened gleefully.
His smile held secrets divine.
He knew she would lead a movement,
Cradled by hands of master design.

The gardener pointed 'round joyfully.
He giggled with earnest delight.
The lark fluttered then perched on his finger.
Stroking her feathers, he spoke with insight:

"You see; freewill is the way to enlightenment.
Like the lark, if held too tight,
Will be crushed in the fear of losing
And a cage only robs one of flight.

"Humanity longs for acceptance
Like a child who is lost in the night.
Cynics weaken faith's purpose,
And shadows blur one of clear sight.

"The lark was chosen for her sweetest of songs,
Her melodies—cheerful and bright.
Her message, to be heard and remembered—
Live together as one, in the light."

Then, interrupted by a gathering crowd—
Curious bystanders from Seneca wondered.
They marveled to witness this epic event,
For divinity and grace swept them under.

She addressed her new allies with confidence,
Cleared her throat to decisively declare:
"The entitlements of men over women
Are privileges which simply aren't fair.

"We too are beings with keen intellect—
Filled with knowledge, contributions, and gifts.
Each one with a divine purpose to fulfill;
Our liberty can no longer be dismissed.

"Our blood runs more patient and caring;
Our tears more humanely flow.
Our compassion and forgiveness, more willing;
We have seeds of morality to sow."

She remembered her sacred promise.
A revolution began on that day.
Her voice, sure and firm, was persuading:
"With pride, we declare equal say.

"We shall lift up the world with our voices.
We'll build dreams of peace and goodwill.
Together, we'll prove ourselves worthy—
A needed balance will then be fulfilled."

The lark's calls quickened in rhythm.
Soon the garden was filled with grand splendors—
As both young and old stood proudly together,
They transformed into freedom's defenders.

Hand in hand, they gathered in more closely,
As the songbird sang hymns of elation.
The crowd listened as her insights were shared,
The Lark's Lesson—a dream for liberation.

"No longer shall your words be rejected.
No longer obedient, dutiful, and meek.
Now you must grow sharp thorns of protection—
Like yellow roses: be powerful and unique.

"With honor, you'll expand this endeavor.
With fortitude, you'll govern with love.
With defiance, your reforms will take root,
For freedom's light radiates from above.

"Your will, now too strong to be broken,
Was birthed in your grandmother's whispers.
The world is in need of your insights—
Now, awaken this charge for all sisters."

"Make a Declaration of Sentiments.
Follow leaders: Anthony, Stanton, and Stone.
Spread seeds of wisdom and enlightenment,
So a new generation of hope can be grown.

"Hasten quickly, to your churches and school yards,
Beyond rivers and mountains that divide.
Build bridges, not walls, to proclaim your rights.
Be empathetic and persistent with pride."

Then the lark took flight in the east wind.
The gardener grinned and nodded her way.
The crowd marched forward to begin this crusade,
For there was no time left for delay.

Yet their message was received with great malice;
Violent fury brewed frenzied alarms.
Swift tempers spread rage of contempt and disdain,
Intimidation left women disarmed.

Squalls of hate stormed about in foolish pride,
Clouded by exploitation and power.
Thunder deafened those who dared to defy,
Domination and chauvinism devoured.

Ever clear in their pursuit for fairness,
Through years of condemning disputes,
The Silent Sentinels endured harsh realities
Of women's restrictions, sufferings, and abuse.

Upon wings of faith, soaring ever higher,
Wives and sisters prevailed day and night.
Standing firm through gales with blistered palms,
Holding banners of white-purple-gold ever tight.

Resilient in their sacred vigil,
Renegades with a purpose to embrace—
No word was ever spoken,
They were adorned by hidden grace.

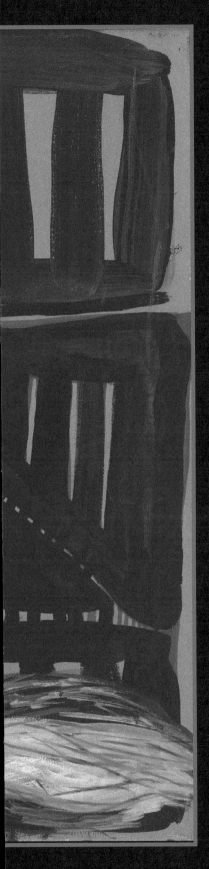

Yet, their efforts were chastised, scorned, and mocked;
Arrogance created torrents of despair.
Relentless abuse from their vicious assaults
Captured the lark in the fowler's snares.

A courageous sacrifice for parity—
Yet they continued to mock, berate and beat.
Her wings were crushed by brutality and wrath—
She lay dead, broken-hearted, at their feet!

*T*hen the gardener reappeared with great sorrow,
His face wrinkled by thousands of suns.
Weeping great tears for this tragedy,
He uttered, "Don't you see what your fears have done?

"The horrors of anger and resentment
And other tortures and nightmares we create,
Are redeemed in the seedlings of tolerance
That sprout forth beyond this garden's gate."

"So who of you, have been hearers and seers
And have done nothing to make things just?
Look deep into your own reflection—
Do you see someone worthy of trust?"

"Are you ready to change your perspective?
Liberty's blessings we all deserve.
You can right this wrong, and amend it—
Claim your voice, seek new laws, and preserve.

"A century from now, you'll be remembered;
The future will embrace this new way.
Still more changes are yet to be considered—
Race, color, and faith will too have their say.

"No doubt, opinions will always differ—
Keep the Golden Rule true, I implore.
Remember the love of the light from above;
Live as equals in harmony evermore."

Then the gardener brushed the dirt from his knees
As he offered a silent prayer.
With a heavy sigh he faced westerly—
Other gardens needed tending elsewhere.

He knew then his promise had been realized,
And gently handed the girl his last seed.
She clutched it close to her heart and sighed,
Its safety was now guaranteed.

"This seed is today but an acorn;
With enough faith it will grow to great height.
The mightiest of mountains can be moved,
If a vision of morality is in sight.

"The lark is the messenger of mercy.
She has left us an endowment—her fairest."
He pointed up toward a mighty oak—
In its branches, a symbol to be cherished.

All eyes then peered slowly upward.
They stood in awe of what lay in her nest.
Three golden eggs resting safely—
Hope, faith and love—her vow manifest.

"So, move forward with nurturing patience.
Your daughters will light the way.
Listen carefully to what they will teach you,
For their insights call forth a new day.

"Please, I beg you, remember the lark's message—
A song of peace meant for everyone.
Bountiful grace and virtue are before us—
Soar together with loving hearts as one."

Section One
Equality of
the United
sex.
Section Two
article
Section

$\mathcal{H}$is shadow vanished ever so slowly
As he reached the horizon's edge.
A new beginning for humanity—
They'd unite in equality's pledge.

Together, ascending to higher ideals,
They sought compromise and fair accord.
With grateful hearts and pure intent,
Integrity had now been restored.

Yesterday's tomorrows are now before us,
A century of sisters stand eternally strong.
Listen—for the song carried faintly on the wind—
The Lesson of the Lark calls us all to belong...

The Nineteenth Amendment
of the United States Constitution

The Nineteenth Amendment to the Constitution

was ratified on August 18, 1920.

It declares that "The right of citizens of the

United States to vote shall not be denied or

abridged by the United States or by any State

on account of gender. Congress shall have power

to enforce this article by appropriate legislation."

Vocabulary Terms

adorned // to decorate or add beauty to

allies // those who support each other for some common purpose

assurance // promise or pledge; certainty; self-confidence

avid // enthusiastic; extremely interested

berated // scold or criticize (someone) angrily

blissful // completely happy and contented

bystanders // a person who is present at an event but not involved in it

cede // to surrender possession of something

chastised // to criticize severely

chauvinism // activity indicative of belief in the superiority of men over women

commitment // a promise or pledge to do something

compromise // a settlement of differences in which each side gives up something

condemnation // an expression of strong disapproval

consciously // with awareness of one's actions

contempt // the feeling that a person or a thing is beneath consideration, worthless, or deserving scorn

corruption // dishonest or illegal actions

crusade // a strong movement to advance a cause or idea

cultivate // to promote growth, to nurture

decisively // in a clear, definite way

declaration // an official statement

defiance // open resistance; bold disobedience

deplorable // shockingly bad in quality

devoured // destroyed or wasted as if by eating

dire // extremely serious or urgent

disdain // intense dislike

divine // sacred

domination // power and control over another person/society.

dutiful // willingly obedient out of a sense of duty and respect

endeavor // a serious attempt or effort

enlightenment // a state of perfect wisdom

ensues // follows as a consequence or a result

entitlement // having a right or claim to something

enveloped // surrounded

exploitation // use of another person or group for selfish purposes

fervency // warmth or intensity of feeling; ardor; zeal; fervor

foreboding // a warning or feeling that something bad will happen

forsaken // abandoned, to turn away entirely

fortitude // courage in facing difficulties

fury // wild or violent anger

gales // very strong winds

hallowed // holy, revered

harsh // extremely unkind or cruel

hasten // move or act quickly

hoisted // raised or lifted

hue // a shade of color

humanely // in a manner marked by compassion, sympathy, or consideration for other human beings or animals

humanity // the human race

imminent // likely to happen; threatening

implore // to beg urgently

integrity // honesty, high moral standards

intimidation // to frighten somebody into doing or not doing something, e.g. by means of violence or blackmail

keen // having or showing eagerness or enthusiasm

liberation // a state of freedom reached after a struggle

magnificent // impressively beautiful, elaborate, or extravagant; striking

malice // ill will, desire to harm others

meek // quiet, gentle, and easily imposed on; submissive

mocked // made fun of

morality // the standards that people use to judge what is right or wrong, good or evil

obedient // doing what is asked or told

opponent // one who goes against

peered // looked closely

persistence // sticking to something; not giving up

persuading // trying to get someone to agree with your plan or opinion

petticoat // a skirt or slip worn under a dress or outer skirt

prevailed // prove more powerful than opposing forces

privileges // special rights; advantages

proclaim // to declare publicly or officially

ratify // to approve, give formal approval to, confirm

redeemed // to do something that makes up for poor behavior or choices

rejected // cast off as valueless

repentance // changing one's mind and actions

reprieve // a temporary relief or delay

resentment // a feeling of deep and bitter anger and ill-will

resilient // quick to recover, bounce back

restriction // rule or regulation that limits something

revolution // a drastic and far-reaching change in ways of thinking and behaving

ridiculed // laughed at; criticized in an embarrassing way

scorned // looked down on; despised

sentiment // a view of or attitude toward a situation or event; an opinion

splendors // things that are very grand or impressive

squalls // strong, violent storms

starched // clothing stiffened and ironed

summon // to call forth; to call together

suffrage // the right to vote

tattered // torn, old, and in generally poor condition; in tatters

threshold // the sill of a doorway; a house's or building's entrance; any point of beginning or entering

tolerance // respecting and accepting others, regardless of their beliefs, practices, or differences

torrents // a violent downpour of rain

trills // to make a quavering or birdlike sound

vigilance // alert watchfulness

virtue // moral excellence

yielded // to give up

Vocabulary Test

1. trills
a. prove more powerful than opposing forces
b. to make a quavering or birdlike sound
c. those who support each other
d. follows as a consequence or a result

2. redeemed
a. prove more powerful than opposing forces
b. a feeling of deep and bitter anger and ill-will
c. torn, old, and in generally poor condition
d. to do something that makes up for poor behavior

3. implore
a. to beg urgently
b. made fun of
c. strong, violent storms
d. to give up

4. fervency
a. warmth or intensity of feeling; ardor; zeal; fervor
b. a warning that something bad will happen
c. scold or criticize (someone) angrily
d. promise or pledge; certainty; self-confidence

5. bystanders
a. a skirt or slip worn under a dress or outer skirt
b. trying to get someone to agree with your plan
c. a settlement of differences
d. a person who is present at an event but not involved in it

6. malice
a. extremely serious or urgent
b. clothing stiffened and ironed
c. ill will, desire to harm others
d. extremely unkind or cruel

7. declaration
a. power and control over another person/society.
b. an official statement
c. to criticize severely
d. a state of perfect wisdom

8. cede
a. destroyed or wasted as if by eating
b. to promote growth, to nurture
c. to surrender possession of something
d. having or showing eagerness or enthusiasm

9. resilient
a. rule or regulation that limits something
b. a temporary relief or delay
c. prove more powerful than opposing forces
d. quick to recover, bounce back

10. ratify
a. to approve, give formal approval to, confirm
b. to make a quavering or birdlike sound
c. to declare publicly or officially
d. those who support each other for some common purpose

11. keen
a. changing one's mind and actions
b. scold or criticize (someone) angrily
c. having or showing eagerness or enthusiasm
d. sticking to something; not giving up

12. vigilance
a. the human race
b. one who goes against
c. moral excellence
d. alert watchfulness

13. defiance
a. open resistance; bold disobedience
b. courage in facing difficulties
c. likely to happen; threatening
d. a temporary relief or delay

14. sentiment
a. a view of or attitude toward a situation or event; an opinion
b. having a right or claim to something
c. the feeling that a person is beneath consideration
d. impressively beautiful, elaborate, or extravagant

15. ensues
a. follows as a consequence or a result
b. things that are very grand or impressive
c. those who support each other
d. laughed at; criticized in an embarrassing way

16. magnificent
a. a view of or attitude toward a situation
b. willingly obedient
c. impressively beautiful, elaborate, or extravagant; striking
d. a settlement of differences

40

17. squalls
a. happy and joyful
b. light and airy
c. strong, violent storms
d. looked down on; despised

18. splendors
a. follows as a consequence or a result
b. a person who is present at an event
c. changing one's mind and actions
d. things that are very grand or impressive

19. hue
a. a state of perfect wisdom
b. having or showing eagerness or enthusiasm
c. extremely serious or urgent
d. a shade of color

20. cultivate
a. honesty, high moral standards
b. dishonest or illegal actions
c. to decorate or add beauty to
d. to promote growth, to nurture

21. condemnation
a. an expression of strong disapproval
b. power and control over another person/society.
c. a serious attempt or effort
d. a promise or pledge to do something

22. liberation
a. use of another person for selfish purposes
b. promise or pledge; certainty; self-confidence
c. a state of freedom reached after a struggle
d. an expression of strong disapproval

23. humanity
a. raised or lifted
b. courage in facing difficulties
c. things that are very grand or impressive
d. the human race

24. dire
a. extremely serious or urgent
b. destroyed or wasted as if by eating
c. to promote growth, to nurture
d. extremely unkind or cruel

25. repentance
a. changing one's mind and actions
b. quick to recover, bounce back
c. open resistance; bold disobedience
d. with awareness of one's actions

26. persuading
a. power and control over another person/society.
b. a view of or attitude toward a situation or event
c. warmth or intensity of feeling; ardor; zeal; fervor
d. trying to get someone to agree with your plan or opinion

27. consciously
a. an expression of strong disapproval
b. with awareness of one's actions
c. having a right or claim to something
d. rule or regulation that limits something

28. persistence
a. changing one's mind and actions
b. quick to recover, bounce back
c. a promise or pledge to do something
d. sticking to something; not giving up

29. avid
a. enthusiastic; extremely interested
b. destroyed or wasted as if by eating
c. to make a quavering or birdlike sound
d. extremely serious or urgent

30. berated
a. scold or criticize (someone) angrily
b. clothing stiffened and ironed
c. to decorate or add beauty to
d. follows as a consequence or a result

31. hallowed
a. torn, old, and in generally poor condition
b. looked closely
c. holy, revered
d. those who support each other

32. privileges
a. honesty, high moral standards
b. a temporary relief or delay
c. quick to recover, bounce back
d. special rights; advantages

33. obedient
a. doing what is asked or told
b. one who goes against
c. a violent downpour of rain
d. likely to happen; threatening

34. starched
a. changing one's mind and actions
b. to decorate or add beauty to
c. quick to recover, bounce back
d. clothing stiffened and ironed

35. enlightenment
a. a promise or pledge to do something
b. a state of perfect wisdom
c. a feeling of deep and bitter anger and ill-will
d. having a right or claim to something

36. scorned
a. scold or criticize (someone) angrily
b. looked down on; despised
c. raised or lifted
d. strong, violent storms

37. forsaken
a. forgotten, abandoned
b. courage in facing difficulties
c. to criticize severely
d. scold or criticize (someone) angrily

38. peered
a. to give up
b. looked closely
c. to decorate or add beauty to
d. scold or criticize (someone) angrily

39. dutiful
a. willingly obedient out of a sense of duty and respect
b. a view of or attitude toward a situation or event
c. a feeling of deep and bitter anger and ill-will
d. ill will, desire to harm others

40. crusade
a. scold or criticize (someone) angrily
b. promise or pledge; certainty; self-confidence
c. warmth or intensity of feeling; ardor; zeal; fervor
d. a strong movement to advance a cause or idea

41. foreboding
a. a warning or feeling that something bad will happen
b. a feeling of deep and bitter anger and ill-will
c. trying to get someone to agree with your plan
d. a promise or pledge to do something

42. assurance
a. a skirt or slip worn under a dress or outer skirt
b. prove more powerful than opposing forces
c. a feeling of deep and bitter anger and ill-will
d. promise or pledge; certainty; self-confidence

43. hoisted
a. to decorate or add beauty to
b. Intense dislike
c. raised or lifted
d. moral excellence

44. exploitation
a. use of another person or group for selfish purposes
b. rule or regulation that limits something
c. things that are very grand or impressive
d. a skirt or slip worn under a dress or outer skirt

45. corruption
a. with awareness of one's actions
b. dishonest or illegal actions
c. an expression of strong disapproval
d. a promise or pledge to do something

46. morality
a. the human race
b. power and control over another person/society.
c. the standards that people use to judge what is right or wrong, good or evil
d. honesty, high moral standards

47. allies
a. those who support each other for some common purpose
b. willingly obedient out of a sense of duty
c. torn, old, and in generally poor condition
d. to make a quavering or birdlike sound

48. devoured
a. scold or criticize (someone) angrily
b. a promise or pledge to do something
c. to decorate or add beauty to
d. destroyed or wasted as if by eating

49. compromise
a. a settlement of differences in which each side gives up something
b. a warning that something bad will happen
c. a view of or attitude toward a situation
d. trying to get someone to agree with your plan

50. virtue
a. moral excellence
b. to give up
c. to beg urgently
d. intense dislike

51. imminent
a. courage in facing difficulties
b. open resistance; bold disobedience
c. scold or criticize (someone) angrily
d. likely to happen; threatening

52. gales
a. extreme happiness
b. easy to get along with
c. very strong winds
d. moral excellence

53. entitlement
a. having a right or claim to something
b. quick to recover, bounce back
c. a state of perfect wisdom
d. changing one's mind and actions

54. ridiculed
a. a feeling of deep and bitter anger and ill-will
b. prove more powerful than opposing forces
c. laughed at; criticized in an embarrassing way
d. to do something that makes up for poor behavior

55. fortitude
a. scold or criticize (someone) angrily
b. completely happy and contented
c. a promise or pledge to do something
d. courage in facing difficulties

56. enveloped
a. moral excellence
b. special rights; advantages
c. cast off as valueless
d. surrounded

57. summon
a. to do something that makes up for poor behavior
b. doing what is asked or told
c. to call forth; to call together
d. to promote growth, to nurture

58. fury
a. warmth or intensity of feeling; ardor; zeal; fervor
b. strong, violent storms
c. wild or violent anger
d. scold or criticize (someone) angrily

59. yielded
a. to beg urgently
b. intense dislike
c. cast off as valueless
d. to give up

60. integrity
a. honesty, high moral standards
b. changing one's mind and actions
c. special rights; advantages
d. a serious attempt or effort

61. disdain
a. the human race
b. intense dislike
c. moral excellence
d. looked closely

62. tattered
a. a skirt or slip worn under a dress or outer skirt
b. a view of or attitude toward a situation or event
c. destroyed or wasted as if by eating
d. torn, old, and in generally poor condition; in tatters

63. threshold
a. the standards that people use to judge what is right or wrong, good or evil
b. the sill of a doorway; a house's or building's entrance; any point of beginning or entering
c. in a manner marked by compassion, sympathy, or consideration for other human beings or animals.
d. things that are very grand or impressive

64. blissful
a. completely happy and contented
b. shockingly bad in quality
c. willingly obedient out of a sense of duty and respect
d. honesty, high moral standards

65. resentment
a. a feeling of deep and bitter anger and ill-will
b. quick to recover, bounce back
c. a settlement of differences in which each side gives up something
d. a skirt or slip worn under a dress or outer skirt

43

66. decisively
   a. a temporary relief or delay
   b. special rights; advantages
   c. in a clear, definite way
   d. shockingly bad in quality

67. endeavor
   a. destroyed or wasted as if by eating
   b. cast off as valueless
   c. a serious attempt or effort
   d. a violent downpour of rain

68. commitment
   a. a promise or pledge to do something
   b. a view of or attitude toward a situation or event; an opinion
   c. a skirt or slip worn under a dress or outer skirt
   d. a state of perfect wisdom

69. domination
   a. an expression of strong disapproval
   b. a feeling of deep and bitter anger and ill-will
   c. rule or regulation that limits something
   d. power and control over another person/society.

70. tolerance
   a. the sill of a doorway; a house's or building's entrance; any point of beginning or entering.
   b. changing one's mind and actions
   c. torn, old, and in generally poor condition
   d. respecting and accepting others, regardless of their beliefs, practices, or differences

71. restriction
   a. a feeling of deep and bitter anger and ill-will
   b. promise or pledge; certainty; self-confidence
   c. dishonest or illegal actions
   d. rule or regulation that limits something

72. mocked
   a. surrounded
   b. to give up
   c. cast off as valueless
   d. made fun of

73. proclaim
   a. quick to recover, bounce back
   b. to declare publicly or officially
   c. a strong movement to advance a cause or idea
   d. prove more powerful than opposing forces

74. meek
   a. having or showing eagerness or enthusiasm
   b. those who support each other for some common purpose
   c. quiet, gentle, and easily imposed on; submissive
   d. to do something that makes up for poor behavior

75. adorned
   a. a temporary relief or delay
   b. to decorate or add beauty to
   c. destroyed or wasted as if by eating
   d. looked down on; despised

76. divine
   a. extremely serious or urgent
   b. looked down on; despised
   c. sacred
   d. evil

77. harsh
   a. looked down on; despised
   b. ill will, desire to harm others
   c. enthusiastic; extremely interested
   d. extremely unkind or cruel

78. torrents
   a. dishonest or illegal actions
   b. honesty, high moral standards
   c. doing what is asked or told
   d. a violent downpour of rain

79. revolution
   a. a state of freedom reached after a struggle
   b. move or act quickly
   c. an official statement
   d. a drastic and far-reaching change in ways of thinking and behaving

80. contempt
   a. the sill of a doorway; a house's or building's entrance; any point of beginning or entering
   b. the feeling that a person or a thing is beneath consideration, worthless, or deserving
   c. the standards that people use to judge what is right or wrong, good or evil
   d. in a manner marked by compassion, sympathy, or consideration for other human beings or animals

81. chauvinism

a. a person who is present at an event but not involved in it
b. a view of or attitude toward a situation or event; an opinion
c. a warning or feeling that something bad will happen
d. activity indicative of belief in the superiority of men over women

82. chastised

a. raised or lifted
b. quick to recover, bounce back
c. one who goes against
d. to criticize severely

83. petticoat

a. a skirt or slip worn under a dress or outer skirt
b. promise or pledge; certainty; self-confidence
c. a warning that something bad will happen
d. a view of or attitude toward a situation or event; an opinion.

84. deplorable

a. dishonest or illegal actions
b. shockingly bad in quality
c. special rights; advantages
d. changing one's mind and actions

85. intimidation

a. respecting and accepting others, regardless of their beliefs, practices, or differences
b. in a manner marked by compassion
c. the standards that people use to judge what is right or wrong, good or evil
d. to frighten somebody into doing or not doing something by means of violence or blackmail

86. prevailed

a. promise or pledge; certainty; self-confidence
b. to do something that makes up for poor behavior
c. scold or criticize (someone) angrily
d. prove more powerful than opposing forces

87. opponent

a. alert watchfulness
b. one who goes against
c. cast off as valueless
d. intense dislike

88. rejected

a. to criticize severely
b. to do something that makes up for poor behavior
c. a serious attempt or effort
d. cast off as valueless

89. humanely

a. power and control over another person/society.
b. to frighten somebody into doing or not doing something
c. in a manner marked by compassion, sympathy, or consideration
d. a person who is present at an event but not involved in it

90. hasten

a. to criticize severely
b. move or act quickly
c. raised or lifted
d. a state of freedom reached after a struggle

Comprehension Study Guide

What is the author's purpose?
To awaken the social charge for equality

What is the central theme of the story?
That tolerance and inclusion lead to peace

Why was it necessary for the Lark to die?
In order for the reader to comprehend the fragility of life

What is the craft and structure of this story?
prose

What is the rhyming pattern for the majority of the text?
A, B, C, B

How many lines per stanza were used?
4

What was the promise made in the garden?
To teach others that their conscience is their guide.

How many points of view are present in the story?
5= lark, girl, gardener, the women, and society

What is the setting of the story?
Seneca Falls, New York in 1848

What is the climax of the story?
When the lark dies

What are the three resolutions of the story?
1. When the gardener gives the girl his last seed

2. When they discover the lark's three golden eggs

3. When the people (men/women) decide to live in peace as equals and show acceptance for diversity of genders.

What was the lark's role in the story?
To be a messenger of mercy

What was the gardener's role in the story?
To be a guide

What was the girl's role in the story?
To spread the light of justice

What is the ERA?
The Equal Rights Amendment

Did the ERA pass? Do women have equal rights as men?
No, it did not pass — No women do not legally have equal rights as men in the United States.

What is the Nineteenth Amendment of the US constitution?
It gives women the legal right to vote.

What is a centennial?
The celebration of 100 years passing.

Why was the gardener relieved that the girl had arrived?
He had been waiting for her, because he knew there was an agent of change on the way.

What happened to the Girl once she entered the garden?
She was given an enchantment of enlightenment.

Why did the lark trust the gardener to sit on his finger?
They were friends in the garden, and had mutual respect for each other.

What did the gardener say the way to enlightenment was?
Freewill

What did the gardener say humanity longs for?
Acceptance

What was the lark's message?
To live together as one, in the light

When the girl addressed the crowd, what did she say about women's liberty?
That it should no longer be dismissed

Why did the lark suggest the women grow sharp thorns like roses?
It's a metaphor for them to protect themselves.

What was the significance of the yellow roses?

They symbolize joy, wisdom, and power. They were worn by the suffragists.

The lark awakened a charge for a woman to do what?

To rise up and become freedom's defenders.

What did the lark mean when she said that their will was too strong to be broken because it was birthed in their grandmother's whispers?

The lark meant that for all of history, women have not had equal rights, and that this is an injustice. She was inferring that change is on the horizon because through the ages, women's voices are becoming stronger and stronger.

Why did the lark want the women to build bridges instead of walls?

The lark was wise enough to see that positive change is best achieved through kindness, pride, and persistence.

Why were the women's messages met with anger?

Society was fearful that women would become too powerful; they were not ready to accept them as equals.

Who were the Silent Sentinels?

A group of women who protested in favor of women's suffrage

What happened to the Silent Sentinels?

Over 2,000 women were harassed, shamed, beaten, arrested, and jailed.

How did the lark die?

The lark died of a broken heart for all of the pain and anguish of every woman.

What did the gardener ask about the lark's death?

"Don't you see what your fears have done?"

From the gardener's perspective who creates horror and resentment?

Each person creates their own fears from within themselves.

How does the gardener say they can be redeemed?

In the seedlings of tolerance that sprout forth in the deeds we demonstrate

What does the gardener mean when he talks about hearers and seers and their reflection?

It comes from the Christian Bible Proverbs 27 and the Hebrew Tanakh. It means that you deceive yourself when you look the other way from injustice.

What is the Golden Rule?

"Treat others the way you would like to be treated". Comes from Christianity, Judaism, Islam, Hinduism, Buddhism, and many other faiths.

What was the significance of the last seed?

It held the chance for tomorrow. If the holder has enough faith in change, then the holder can do the impossible. This comes from Matthew 17:20.

What gift did the lark leave?

Three golden eggs: hope, faith, and love. This comes from the Bible Corinthians 13

What is carried faintly on the wind?

The song of the lark which unites all

Why is this story called the Lesson of the Lark?

The lark's character is the one that brings resolution to the story through her words and actions.

Comprehension Test

1. What is the rhyming pattern for the majority of the book?
a. A, A, B, B
b. A, B, C, D
c. A, B, C, B
d. A, B, A, B

2. What is a centennial?
a. A person who stands guard
b. The celebration of 100 years passing
c. A little more than one penny
d. An insect with 100 legs

3. Why was it necessary for the lark to die?
a. In order for the reader to comprehend the fragility of life
b. So the swan could go free
c. The winter frost was coming.
d. So that the loon would sing her songs of sorrow

4. What did the lark mean when she said, "Your will is too strong to be broken because it was birthed in their grandmother's whispers?
a. The lark was telling them to speak up because their grandmothers couldn't hear well.
b. The lark was inferring that change is on the horizon because through the ages women's voices are becoming stronger and more confident with each new generation.
c. The lark meant that the women would have babies with super-power strength.
d. The lark was happy that the grandmothers were quiet.

5. What is the Nineteenth Amendment of the US constitution?
a. It permits people the right to sing and dance when they want to.
b. It gives women the legal right to vote.
c. It allows everyone to marry who they want.
d. It grants everyone three wishes.

6. Why were the women's messages for equality met with anger and resentment?
a. Those who were opposed to equal rights thought women were bossy and ignorant.
b. They thought their messages were hard to understand because they were in pig Latin.
c. Society was fearful that women would become too powerful; they were not ready to accept them as equals.
d. They thought the women were lying.

7. The lark awakened a charge for women to do what?
a. To stop arguing about the cost of tea in China
b. To become hot dog vendors on the streets
c. To live together as one, in the light
d. To take more time to play chess

8. What was the significance of the yellow roses?
a. Yellow roses are often used at funerals and mean death
b. They are grown in the Artic and are important food for polar bears
c. To remind everyone to smile and be happy
d. They were worn by the suffragists and symbolize joy, wisdom, and power.

9. What is the central theme of the story?
a. That tolerance and inclusion lead to peace
b. Eat more pancakes
c. Be nice
d. Larks prefer to live in gardens

10. What is the Golden Rule?
a. He who has the gold, makes the rules
b. "Treat others the way you would like to be treated". This originates from Christianity, Judaism, Islam, Hinduism, Buddhism, and many other faiths.
c. Don't wear gold on Mondays
d. A measuring device that is made of solid gold

11. What was the gardener's role in the story?
a. To pull the weeds
b. To be a guide
c. To feed the lark
d. To help with the composting

12. How did the lark die?
   a. She died of a broken heart for all of the pain and anguish of every woman.
   b. She had a fight with a raven.
   c. She got stuck in a storm drain.
   d. She ate some rotten worms.

13. What was the lark's message?
   a. To make your problems turn into rainbows
   b. To never play Angry Birds
   c. To live together as one, in the light
   d. To never sit on wet electrical wires

14. Why did the lark suggest the women grow sharp thorns like roses?
   a. To poke people when they're mean
   b. It's a joke; the lark knows women can't grow thorns.
   c. To get back at their enemies
   d. It's a metaphor for the women to protect themselves.

15. What is the craft and structure of this story?
   a. Lyrics
   b. Prose
   c. Limerick
   d. Riddle

16. What did the gardener say the way to enlightenment was?
   a. Sun bathing
   b. Freewill
   c. Light bulbs
   d. Photosynthesis

17. What was the promise made in the garden?
   a. To always do her homework
   b. To never ride a bike without a helmet
   c. To teach others that their conscience is their guide
   d. To show others how to make Cuban sandwiches

18. What was the significance of the last seed?
   a. There would be no more Truffula Trees
   b. The girl ate the rest when she carved out her pumpkin.
   c. Maybe the gardener had more, but he was just kidding.
   d. It held the chance for tomorrow. If the holder has enough faith in change, then the holder can do the impossible. This comes from the Bible book of Matthew 17:20.

19. From the gardener's perspective, who creates horror and resentment?
   a. Each person creates their own fears from within themselves.
   b. Anyone who wears clown suits
   c. People who try to sneak into his garden
   d. Big Foot and the Loch Ness Monster

20. What does the gardener mean when he talks about hearers and seers and their reflection?
   a. Some people can't hear or see.
   b. It comes from the Bible Proverbs 27 and the Hebrew Tanakh. It means that you deceive yourself when you look the other way from injustice.
   c. Broken mirrors are bad luck.
   d. Water reflects light and sound.

21. What was the lark's role in the story?
   a. To be a messenger of mercy
   b. To eat Twinkies and be joyful
   c. To fly south as soon as the snow strikes
   d. To cause trouble

22. How many lines per stanza were used?
   a. 4
   b. 2
   c. 6
   d. 5

23. What is the author's purpose?
   a. To eat more pie
   b. To jump off a cliff
   c. To awaken the social charge for equality
   d. To laugh in the face of adversity

24. What happened to the Silent Sentinels?

a. They were given three golden eggs: hope, faith, and love.

b. They ate acorns.

c. They moved to an island.

d. They were over 2,000 women who were were harassed, shamed, beaten, arrested, and jailed for protesting.

25. What does the ERA stand for?

a. The Equal Rights Amendment

b. The Everybody's Rights Agreement

c. The Equal Random Assessment

d. The Even Rates Accord

26. How many points of view are present in the story?

a. 2 = The gardener and the girl

b. 3 = The gardener, the girl, and the lark

c. 1 = society

d. 5 = lark, girl, gardener, the women, and society

27. Why did the lark want the women to build bridges instead of walls between the men?

a. Bridges are cheaper to build.

b. Bridges are fun to cross over.

c. The lark was wise enough to see that positive change is best achieved through kindness, pride, and persistence.

d. Walls crumble faster.

28. What gift did the lark leave?

a. A pink tutu

b. Three golden eggs: hope, faith, and love. This comes from the Bible Corinthians 13

c. A box of chocolates

d. A bronze medal

29. How does the gardener say they can be redeemed?

a. If they just say they are sorry

b. In the seedlings of tolerance that sprout forth in the deeds we demonstrate

c. If they run away from their problems

d. If they go to the cave near the castle

30. Who were the Silent Sentinels?

a. Guards who stand on the tower of London

b. Monks who are quiet

c. A group of women who protested in favor of women's suffrage

d. Schools of fish that swim up river

31. What are the three resolutions of the story?

a. Peanut butter, jelly, and Wonder bread

b. Earth, Wind, and Fire

c. Peace, love, and Rock n' Roll

d. When the gardener gives the girl his last seed, when they discover the lark's three golden eggs, and when the people (men/women) decide to live in peace as equals and show acceptance for diversity

32. What happened to the girl once she entered the garden?

a. She turned into a frog.

b. She was given the enchantment of enlightenment.

c. She slipped and fell into the river.

d. She grew into a giant.

33. What is carried faintly on the wind?

a. The song of the lark which unites all

b. A bad smell from a landfill

c. The smell of chocolate chip cookies

d. The sound of train whistles

34. Did the ERA pass? Do women have equal rights as men?

a. Yes! By a long shot!

b. No, it did not pass - No women do not legally have equal rights as men in the United States.

c. Yes, but just barely

d. No, now it never can

35. What was the role of the girl in the story?

a. To become a soccer star

b. To own a potato chip factory

c. To spread the light of justice

d. To save homeless cats

36. Why is this story called the Lesson of the Lark?

a. The lark spoke of the importance of eating your vegetables.

b. The lark learned from the girl.

c. The lark's character is the one that brings resolution to the story through her words and actions.

d. The lark taught Spanish in her spare time.

37. Why was the gardener relieved that the girl had arrived?

a. He was tired of doing all of the gardening himself.

b. He had been waiting for her, because he knew there was an agent of change on the way.

c. He knew it was her turn to rake.

d. She paid him money for his work.

38. What is the climax of the story?
   a. When the girl enters the garden
   b. When the gardener leaves
   c. When the crowd of women set out on their crusade
   d. When the lark dies

39. When the girl addressed the crowd, what did she say about women's liberty?
   a. That it should no longer be dismissed
   b. That they needed to join a rock band to seek justice
   c. She told them the Statue of Liberty had been painted purple.
   d. She said it was time to do the polka.

40. What is the setting of the story?
   a. Kingstown, Jamaica in 2015
   b. Seneca Falls, New York in 1848
   c. Paris, France in 1960
   d. Wellington, New Zealand in 2018

41. What did the gardener ask about the lark's death?
   a. How could you do it?
   b. Why have you forsaken me?
   c. Don't you see what your fears have done?
   d. Wow! She wasn't that old.

42. What did the gardener say humanity longs for?
   a. Ice cream
   b. A great movie
   c. Acceptance
   d. To be popular

43. Why did the lark trust the gardener to sit on his finger?
   a. The lark didn't want to hurt the gardener's feelings.
   b. The gardener taught the lark to mimic him.
   c. They were friends in the garden, and had mutual respect for each other.
   d. Larks sit on peoples' fingers all the time.

1. The image on page 15 shows the girl with many arms. Where do they all come from?

2. On page 18, what are the three buildings?

3. What are the symbols on the girl's bloomers in the image on page 15?

4. What was the illustrator trying to convey on page 26 by including the hands from Sandy Hook and the flowers from Columbine?

5. On page 24, why did the illustrator include the 911 reflecting pool memorial?

6. In the image on page 34, what do the broken handcuffs and the open bird cage represent?

7. What are all of the names written in the middle of the image on page 19?

Essay Questions

1. Describe the garden using sensory language to provide details of what the experience of the enchantment would have been like from the perspective of the girl? Write this in first person perspective.

2. How did the lark know all that she knew? Who had she learned her wisdom from? Where did the lark come from? How did the lark have the magical powers to speak?

3. Imagine a conversation between the lark and the gardener? Use dialogue to describe what they might have talked about during their times in the garden? What would they express about their concerns for the world?

4. Write an extended ending to the story. What events would unfold naturally given the details already presented. What would happen once the golden eggs hatch? What would happen once the acorn is planted? Would the gardener ever return? What would happen to the girl as she ages?

5. Add a new character to the story who is an antagonist. What would they do or say? What kind of trouble could they stir up? What new problems would they create?

6. The saying; "It's better to build bridges than walls," originates from the African proverb; "The wise build bridges — and the foolish build walls." It was recently used in the film Black Panther. What do you think this means? What can this phrase be related to it? What are the ramifications of building either?

7. Imagine you are a 20-year-old female living in the 1850's in a large city in the United States. You are unmarried, have graduated from high school, and work in a factory. You hope to be promoted for your hard work. You live with your family in a very small apartment, and give them most of the money you earn just to help your family to survive. Both your father and your boss are against equal rights for women. Would you risk getting kicked out of your home or fired to help support the cause?

8. Pretend you are a 35-year-old female living in 1900 in a small farm town in the United States. You are married and have four small children. You did not finish high school and are unable to read. You are a homemaker and feed your family from a garden and a few livestock. Your husband is opposed to equal rights. The ladies in the village are forming a club to petition for equal rights. Would you secretly attend the meetings knowing that if your husband found out that it could break up your family?

19th Amendment and Women's Suffrage Video Link References

2:20 **19th Amendment – History Channel**
https://www.history.com/topics/womens-history/19th-amendment

4:32 **Dolly Parton 19th Amendment**
http://tasteofcountry.com/dolly-parton-a-womans-right/

2:59 **School House Rock - Sufferin till Suffrage**
https://www.youtube.com/watch?v=CGHGDO_b_qo

3:49 **1910s-Women's Suffrage and Equal Rights**
https://www.youtube.com/watch?v=AZxaHvwPwNo

2:19 **One Woman: One Vote**
https://www.youtube.com/watch?v=ycWEnqhHFBE

2:50 **Sound Smart: Women's Suffrage**
https://www.youtube.com/watch?v=HGEMscZE5dY

3:03 **Not for Ourselves Alone**
https://www.pbs.org/video/womens-suffrage-7neirw/

6:46 **Two examples of National Suffrage**
https://www.pbs.org/video/two-examples-national-suffragist-dyp1zl/

2:15 **Iron Jawed Angels Preview (Not appropriate for younger students)**
https://www.youtube.com/watch?time_continue=135&v=StF3_MjotBg

Take Action!

When you purchase this book, a portion of the proceeds will go towards the ERA through the Equal-Means-Equal campaign. For more information, please go to lauraknightcobb.com.

Test Keys

Vocabulary Test Key

1.	B	54.	C
2.	D	55.	D
3.	A	56.	D
4.	A	57.	C
5.	D	58.	C
6.	C	59.	D
7.	B	60.	A
8.	C	61.	B
9.	D	62.	D
10.	A	63.	B
11.	C	64.	A
12.	D	65.	A
13.	A	66.	C
14.	A	67.	C
15.	A	68.	A
16.	C	69.	D
17.	C	70.	D
18.	D	71.	D
19.	D	72.	D
20.	D	73.	B
21.	A	74.	C
22.	C	75.	B
23.	D	76.	C
24.	A	77.	D
25.	A	78.	D
26.	D	79.	D
27.	B	80.	B
28.	D	81.	D
29.	A	82.	D
30.	A	83.	A
31.	C	84.	B
32.	D	85.	D
33.	A	86.	D
34.	D	87.	B
35.	B	88.	D
36.	B	89.	C
37.	A	90.	B
38.	B		
39.	A		
40.	D		
41.	A		
42.	D		
43.	C		
44.	A		
45.	B		
46.	C		
47.	A		
48.	D		
49.	A		
50.	A		
51.	D		
52.	C		
53.	A		

Comprehension Test Key

1.	C
2.	B
3.	A
4.	B
5.	B
6.	C
7.	C
8.	D
9.	A
10.	B
11.	B
12.	A
13.	C
14.	D
15.	B
16.	B
17.	C
18.	D
19.	A
20.	B
21.	A
22.	A
23.	C
24.	D
25.	A
26.	D
27.	C
28.	B
29.	B
30.	C
31.	D
32.	B
33.	A
34.	B
35.	C
36.	C
37.	B
38.	D
39.	A
40.	B
41.	C
42.	C
43.	C

The Illustrations ... A Closer Look Key

1. She is depicting Durga, a fierce warrior goddess in Hindu art who battles against evil.

2. A Christian Church, a Buddhist Temple, and a Muslim Mosque.

3. They are religious symbols representing many different faiths including; Christian, Islamic, Jewish, Shinto, Paganism, Ankh, and Bahai.

4. To demonstrate that resentment and anger lead to horrific results; so that the reader would see the connection between fury and destruction in order to emphasize the need for compassion and love

5. To show the severity of what hate and fear can do to society; to remind us how fragile life is; to awaken the degree of seriousness for freedom

6. Women gaining the right to vote, and foreshadows the equality and liberation to come

7. They are the names of some of the attendees the Seneca Falls Convention.

About the Author

LAURA KNIGHT COBB is an author, lyricist and poet. She lives in Traverse City, Michigan with her husband of 25 years. She is a proud mother of two remarkable young adults. As a teacher of 25 years, she has educated students in every grade K-8 in; Florida, England, Texas, Switzerland, Michigan, and Scotland. She received an honorary Fulbright award, and earned Summa Cum Laude with a Master's Degree in Curriculum and Instruction. She is a published poet with the American Anthology of Poetry. She is also a lyricist. Her work, "The Promise of Peace" was performed at Carnegie Hall in New York city. She also wrote Prose to accompany the musical score for "The 11th Hour." Laura considers this is an evolutionary time in history. She is steadfast in the belief that we are all connected and that our purpose is to share our gifts as positive agents of change in the world. Please go to lauraknightcobb.com for more information.

About the Illustrator

The illustrator is MAYA JAMES. Maya is a storyteller, illustrator, spoken word poet, organizing activist, and political multimedia artist currently residing in Traverse City, Michigan. Her works range from storytelling on "Risk!" episode #639 'Survivors' to The New York Times Race/Related, to the Portland Poetry Slam of 2013 and with the infamous Climbing PoeTree during their Hagerty Center performance in 2015. She was a headliner at 'Hybrid', an exhibition at Twisted Fish Gallery in Elk Rapids, Michigan. She was responsible for organizing and hosting "What's Real: Being Gay in Black America"; a night of comedy that united, publicized and funded social justice, primarily LGBTQIA groups in the Northern Michigan area. Maya was a delegate for the Bernie Sanders campaign, and will continue to deliver speeches at community organizations about all forms of social injustice, but particularly the #blacklivesmatter movement. Maya's newest collection "This Woman Believes: and Other Untold Stories" was featured during Artprize 2018 at the Grand Rapids African American Museum and Archives.

CPSIA information can be obtained
at www.ICGtesting.com
Printed in the USA
BVHW020356171019
561330BV00003B/7/P